CH00547565

© Day One Publications 2010
First printed 2010

ISBN 978-1-84625-204-4
Scripture quotations taken from the
HOLY BIBLE, NEW INTERNATIONAL VERSION.
Copyright © 1973, 1978, 1984 by International Bible Society.
Used by permission of Hodder & Stoughton Publishers,
A member of the Hodder Headline Group.
All rights reserved.
"NIV" is a registered trademark of International Bible Society.
UK trademark number 1448790.

British Library Cataloguing in Publication Data available

Published by Day One Publications
Ryelands Road, Leominster, HR6 8NZ
TEL 01568 613 740 FAX 01568 611 473
email—sales@dayone.co.uk
web site—www.dayone.co.uk

Designed by Kathryn Chedgzoy and printed by Orchard Press, Cheltenham Ltd.

Helen Clark

Esther:
God's invisible hand

Pocket
Bible People

DayOne

Contents

' . . . If we are Christians, we should not believe in coincidences. Nothing happens by accident. '

 *Introduction*

Esther is one of those books nestled in the middle of the Old Testament and is therefore often overlooked. If you have heard of Esther in church, you may recall her story going something like this:

• Poor, pretty Jewish girl gets chosen by tall, powerful king to be his queen.

• Nasty, evil advisor to the king tricks the king into ordering the killing of all Jews in his land.

• Queen, with help of wise cousin, hatches a plan to trick nasty, evil advisor and persuade king to reverse order.

• Nasty, evil advisor is himself put to death and king, queen and cousin all live happily ever after in palace.

Sounds a bit like a pantomime, doesn't it? You can imagine the audience shouting to Esther, 'He's behind you!'

I always had a romantic notion of Esther being tucked away in a palace with

a handsome, powerful husband. Everything in her life was easy, and she was surrounded by luxury; but if you actually read the book of Esther you soon realize that my childhood ideas of this woman were completely wrong and her story was no pantomime!

The real deal!

In reality, by the time we start reading her story, Esther had already lost her parents. She was taken away from her loving older cousin and made to live among strangers, many of whom would not have been pleasant to her. She had to live with the constant threat of being put to death by her own husband if she put one foot wrong.

Esther faced a powerful advisor who hated her Jewish race with a passion and was strong enough to command the whole race to be killed. Only with her cousin's advice did Esther manage to prevent this awful tragedy. During all this time, her own life would have been very much at risk, too!

It now sounds a bit more like a thriller than a pantomime, doesn't it?

What have I missed out?

Re-read the paragraphs above and you will notice that there is something—or someone, I should say—I have made no mention of. Even if you have never read the book of Esther and have no idea who she was, it shouldn't be too difficult for you to work it out.

Remember, Esther was in the Bible, God's book. For a book to be in the Bible it has to be about God and his love for us. It has to contain God's plan to save his people from their enemies and from their own sin. So where is God in this story?

He's not there, but he clearly is!

Believe it or not, God's name is not mentioned anywhere in the book of Esther. It is the only Bible book to have that claim to fame.

However, just because his name isn't mentioned anywhere, it does not mean that God wasn't working behind the scenes throughout the whole story. Hopefully, I will be able to show you how and where.

To help you right at the start, I want to remind you of a subject that I mentioned in my previous books on Ruth and Simon Peter—**'coincidence'**.

If we are Christians, we should not believe in coincidences. Nothing happens by accident. There are many times in Esther's story where you might be tempted to think, 'What an amazing coincidence that so and so came along or such and such happened at just the right time!' Whenever you are tempted to think like that, try to stop your train of thought and realize that that was when God was working behind the scenes.

For example: Think of your favourite movie. I have to confess that mine is, and always will be, any of the *Star Wars* movies. I have always enjoyed the stories, the battleships, the action and the strange creatures. And always had a soft spot for Chewbacca and the Ewoks, as they are so cute and furry! But back to the point before I get carried away.

It wasn't until recently, when I watched a documentary on the making of the first three *Star Wars* movies (for you movie buffs, episodes 4, 5 and 6), that I started to appreciate how much work and preparation had gone on behind the scenes of these movies. I had taken them for granted for so many years and had never fully appreciated the huge role played by George Lucas in putting everything together.

In the story of Esther, God's name doesn't get a mention, but his direction behind the scenes is clear for anyone to see. Let's take a look at it together.

Think tank

1. The book of Esther has only ten chapters, so try to read the whole of that book before you carry on reading this book, so that you can get an overview of the story. Test me: see if you can find God mentioned by name in any of the ten chapters. (Note: Esther is the seventeenth book in the Old Testament and is sandwiched between Nehemiah and Job.)

2. Try now to get into the habit of not believing in coincidences. If something unusual or amazing happens, try to look for God's hand in that situation. It will be there. Trust him.

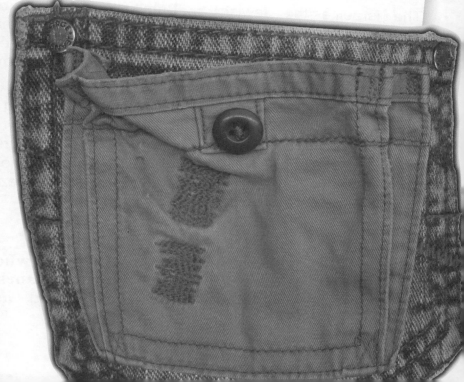

'. . . It is good to learn about what is going on in our world and to pray for countries and peoples who are having a really hard time.'

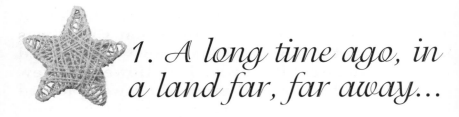

1. A long time ago, in a land far, far away...

... there was a history lesson

I'm sorry, but it has to be done. This story could get quite confusing if you don't understand the history behind it and how we get to Esther's point in time. This section will answer a lot of questions that may crop up later, but I will be as brief as I can.

Here are the headlines!

- The Israelites/the Jewish race had been wicked and had rebelled against God time and time again. He had given them their own land and blessed them, but they had turned their backs on him and his messengers

- God allowed a king called Nebuchadnezzar of the Babylonians to take ov the land of Israel, and ma Jews were taken into exi far away from their home

- After seventy years, G allowed Cyrus, king Persia, to overthrow t Babylonians, and he rul over all the land previous taken by Nebuchadnezz

Note 1: 'Exile' here means that the Jews who survived were taken by force to the victors' (Babylonians') homeland and were used as servants.

Note 2: It was probably thanks to Daniel (of 'Daniel and the lions' den' fame) that Cyrus was lenient with the Jews and that they were allowed to return to Israel if they wished. However, a few generations had passed since they were forced into exile, and many had made homes in their new land. So many decided to stay put and Cyrus was a fair king, allowing them to live in peace and follow their own faith, which by this time was returning. For now, the Jews had learnt their lesson.

The Persian Empire ruled for many years, and as the first scene opens in Esther chapter 1, we read that Xerxes, son of Darius and grandson of Cyrus, was ruler over 127 provinces. The year was 483 bc (Before Christ).

Where are Babylon and Persia today?

You may have heard of the name 'Babylon' before. In fact, I think most people know it from an old Boney M song, *The Rivers of Babylon*. If you don't know this song, then I guarantee that your parents will. However, neither Persia nor Babylon exists today.

To give you some idea of where they were, you will need a world map. The Babylonian Empire was taken over by the Persian Empire, so they really refer to the same area. These empires were huge.

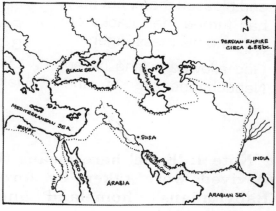

Find the following countries on a map: Turkey, Iraq, Iran, Pakistan, Jordan, Lebanon, Israel. The Persian Empire covered all these countries. Not only that, it also included parts of Egypt, Sudan, Libya, Afghanistan, and the whole of Syria and Kuwait. It was an enormous area, so you can imagine that the king of this empire was incredibly powerful.

The king's main palace was in the capital of this empire, a place called Susa, which is in the south-west of modern-day Iran. It was at this palace that most of the action in Esther took place.

Cyrus was the king who had carried out all those incredible, successful invasions to build up the empire, so you can imagine that Xerxes felt he had a lot to live up to. They were huge shoes to fill.

Think tank

1. The Jewish people have a very rough history. Their periods of peace seem to have always been short-lived. Can you think of a recent time in their history when they were forced to flee their countries (in Europe) or risk being taken by force?

If you don't know, ask any relative who is over sixty-five years old, as this person will have lived through that period.

In another of my books I mentioned a lady called Corrie ten Boom. She experienced being taken away by force and had to endure awful conditions in a concentration camp, where she lost her father and sister. If you haven't read her story, I recommend you read it or watch the film of her life, *The Hiding Place*.

2. Even today the Jewish people are going through a long period of unrest in Israel because of their conflict with the Palestinians. I won't go into the rights or wrongs of either side, but I would encourage you to look into it for yourself. It is good to learn about what is going on in our world and to pray for countries and peoples who are having a really hard time. It also makes us appreciate it even more when our countries are going through peaceful times.

'. . . this was no ordinary banquet. '

2. Act One, Scene One

Read Esther 1:1–22

The book starts with Xerxes (who was also known by his Hebrew name, Ahasuerus) holding a banquet for all the princes, nobles and military officials in all of his provinces. But this was no ordinary banquet, for the following reasons:

• For a start, remember that there were 127 provinces, and there would have been more than just one representative from each province. That would make a lot of people.

• The banquet lasted 180 days. That is almost six months, which is a long time! Not all the representatives would necessarily have stayed for the whole six months, but it would still have been a very busy time. Granted, they would also not have been simply eating and drinking the whole time. They would have had a lot of business matters to discuss and probably further invasions to plan. Xerxes clearly had a lot of wealth to show off to all these officials, but the eating and drinking would have been part of that. Then, at the end at that banquet, there was eating and drinking for another seven days!

It all sounds rather obscene to me. Read verses 6–7. It was all very over-the-top. There would have been people in Xerxes' provinces who could not afford their next meal, and yet there he was, showing off about how much he owned!

Why did he hold the banquet? *(verses 1–6)*

The main reason seems to be that Xerxes wanted to show off all his wealth and splendour. As I mentioned in the Introduction, his grandfather Cyrus had ruled well and had been very successful in taking over many lands. I suspect that Xerxes had a bit of an inferiority complex and felt that he had to prove something in his own right. His father had been dead for two years and perhaps he wanted to let everyone know that he was now in charge and had himself done well during these two years.

I think the sin of pride had a serious part to play, but are we any different?

For example: Think of the obsession we have with designer labels. At school it is vital that you are seen to be wearing the right brand of clothes or have the most up-to-date technical equipment. Your status in life is often measured by what you have, not by the sort of person you are. And yet there are many families who struggle to buy the weekly food shop, never mind a designer label.

Little has really changed from Xerxes' day, and we are all to blame.

Don't get me wrong here. It is nice to have lovely stuff, and there is nothing wrong with that if your parents can afford it, but it is vital that we realize that what we own means nothing compared with being kind and generous to others. Don't get too caught up in it all, as Xerxes did. Squash that pride.

Do you think that God cares that you have the latest football colours of your favourite team? No, he cares more about how you treat others and look out for them.

Back to the banquet! *(verses 7–8)*

We now come to a subject that will soon become a big issue in your life, if it has not done so already.

We are told that Xerxes encouraged his guests to drink as much wine as they wanted. When it says in verse 8 that he allowed each guest to drink in his own way, it refers to a custom of the day. In those days, it was not acceptable to drink before your host, or to drink more than your host, especially if your host was the king. But at this banquet, guests were allowed to ignore that order and could go ahead and drink to their hearts' content. As you can imagine, there would have been some very drunk people at that banquet.

Message for today

Christians differ on the subject of whether or not drinking alcohol is OK. There are mainly two camps:

Camp One: No alcohol at all

Christians in this camp worry about leading others astray. There are people who have serious addictions to alcohol, or may develop such addictions in the future. These Christians feel that if a person who is struggling

with alcohol sees them openly drinking, they may think that their problem is not so serious after all and may be led down the wrong route. These Christians do not want to be bad examples to anyone.

Camp Two: Alcohol in moderation

Christians in this camp see nothing wrong with drinking alcohol in small quantities. There are actually medical benefits to drinking half a glass or one glass of alcohol a day. These Christians think that alcohol is only a problem when you drink too much—i.e., when your thoughts and actions are affected and it is clear to everyone around you that you are 'drunk'.

Both camps agree that drinking too much is not right for a Christian. We are called to always have our wits about us and to always be ready and willing to witness for Christ and set a good example. A drunk Christian will never be a good witness for Christ!

The first queen in a supporting role (verses 9–12)

At the start of the book of Esther we see that Xerxes was married to a woman called Vashti. Her name suited her well:

Vashti means **'beautiful'**, and she really was!

She was tucked away holding her own banquet for the women when Xerxes, 'in high spirits from wine' (i.e., drunk, verse 8) thought that it would be a great idea to order her to get dressed up in the family jewels and parade herself in front of his guests.

Vashti refused to attend.

An unfair reputation

As a young child, I always felt that Vashti was wrong to refuse to come to the king when he called and must have been very disobedient, but looking at the passage now, I have changed my mind. Although historians lead us to believe that she was not a particularly nice woman, and we don't know the motives for her refusal, I actually admire her stand for the following reasons:

- She would have known that, after seven days of drinking, the men would all be seriously affected by alcohol. For her to parade in front of them while they were in this state would not have been wise. Perhaps she was concerned about what else the men would ask her to do once she arrived. People generally do not behave well when they are drunk, and things that they would never normally consider all of a sudden seem to be good ideas. Usually, these 'good ideas' are never good ideas. Vashti may have felt quite threatened.

- She knew that refusing the king in front of guests would have serious consequences for her. You just didn't refuse the king—ever! She was very courageous.

- She was hosting her own banquet, and the king knew that. It would have been quite rude for her to have left her own guests.

She paid dearly! (verses 13–22)

We have already established that Xerxes was a very proud man. Now he had been shown up in front of the most important people in the empire apart from himself! A woman, his wife, had refused an order in front of his guests. This was very embarrassing for him. It's no surprise that he did not let her get away with it.

Xerxes called together a select few 'wise men' to get their advice on what to do with Vashti, and they all advised that she should never see the king again and that her title of queen should be taken away (verse 19). Basically, they were to divorce, but Vashti would have no say in this whatsoever.

Note: You probably realize this already, but women in Esther's day were very much the underdogs. They did not have rights of their own but had to obey their husbands in everything, and that is the way the men wanted to keep it.

What amazes me is that Xerxes had to ask people's advice at all. He was the king and could do whatever he saw fit. His need to ask what the law stated suggests that he was quite weak in character and was easily influenced. This character flaw comes up time and time again, but God would even use it for good by the end of the story.

Whether or not Xerxes was still drunk when he had this conversation with the wise men, we don't know. We are not sure whether it was the drink, his pride, or a bit of both that made him think they had spoken wisely, but he agreed with everything they said.

A bit harsh, don't you think?

I think this decision was very harsh, but remember, God's plan was unfolding and it had to be this way for future developments and for the saving of his people to take place.

The real reason for the wise men advising the king in this way is quite clear. They were probably not particularly bothered that Vashti had disobeyed the king, and I doubt they were at all concerned about his welfare or reputation. They were more worried about their own households and the example she had set for others (verse 18). They had their own wives safely under their control and they didn't want them getting the idea from Vashti that they could also disobey their husbands. Vashti had to be made into an example that clearly showed that no woman could get away with disobeying an order from her husband.

What became of Vashti no one knows, as she is never mentioned again, but I think she made a wiser, braver decision than people have given her credit for.

So we leave the king angry and queen-less, and with his pride seriously dented! This chapter does not end on a happy note at all. Can you see God working behind the scenes? Maybe not yet, but he is certainly there. Be patient, and all will be revealed as Esther makes her first appearance.

Think tank

1. For those of you who are blessed in having parents who can afford to buy you designer clothes or expensive equipment, don't be proud. It doesn't make you any more special than those without these things, especially in God's eyes.

2. Please consider the issue of alcohol carefully. I am not going to tell you which of the two camps you should be in, but for your own safety, please do not get into the habit

of drinking too much once you are of legal age. Alcohol does seriously affect the choices you make when you are under its influence, and you really could get into a lot of trouble and make very unwise decisions.

Some girls are taken advantage of and raped while they are drunk and do not have the awareness to stop it. It happens. Innocent people die when people drive under the influence of alcohol. Friendships are ruined because people, while drunk, say things that they would never normally say in public. The gentlest of men can get into fights when they are drunk, as they react to things so differently.

Alcohol can seriously affect your personality and your life. Please think seriously about this issue and don't bend to peer pressure. It is not worth it. A proper friend will respect your decision not to get drunk. Show them that you can enjoy yourself without the need for alcohol.

3. Look back through this chapter and see if you can write down all the sins that Xerxes was guilty of during Esther chapter 1. Here is a list that I came up with, but try to do it for yourself first and then see if we agree:

- pride
- drinking too much alcohol
- asking his wife to do something that was not loving or caring for her personal welfare
- weakness; easily influenced, did not know his own mind
- bad temper.

Wow! This man needed help. Look through the list and be honest about whether you are also guilty of any or all of these sins. Ask God to forgive you and help you work on these areas of your life so that you can behave in a better way.

' . . . And we know that in all things God works for the good of those who love him. '

(Romans 8 v 28)

3. Enter the star of the show

Read Esther 2:1–18

We are not told how long the interval was between chapters 1 and 2 of the book of Esther, but historical writers from the time would suggest that four years had passed. We know that Xerxes was busy trying to invade and conquer Greece soon after Vashti was deposed. However, he was unsuccessful, so that would not have helped his mood.

You can imagine Xerxes returning to the palace and not having a wife to comfort and console him on his disastrous war. No wonder chapter 2 starts with Xerxes sounding as if he was regretting his rash decision to banish Queen Vashti. This is not said in so many words, but we do read that his anger had subsided and that he remembered Vashti and the whole incident. This carries a definite suggestion of regret and depression.

It was not in his personal attendants' best interests to allow the king to stay in this mood—it is more than likely that these were the very men who had suggested banishing Vashti in the first place. They would not have wanted Xerxes' anger to return and be aimed at them instead.

So they came up with a fabulous plan! *(verses 2–4)*

Their plan was to bring lots of beautiful women into the harem, or women's house. Each one was to get one night with the king to impress him. Whoever pleased him the most would be chosen as the new queen.

This sounds to me like a beauty pageant more than a 'let's-choose-a-wife-that-will-be-a-comfort-and-support-to-you' pageant, but Xerxes seemed to like the idea of choosing a woman to replace Vashti who was even more beautiful than her.

If Vashti had been the unpleasant woman that history would suggest, we might think that Xerxes would have wanted to spend time getting to know her replacement first and so choose her more for her wonderful personality, but no ... Sometimes people never learn. Xerxes again behaved impulsively, and immediately the search began.

Not the way God intended!

If you are reading this and wondering about the morals of the whole thing, you would be completely right. You can brush if off by saying, 'Well, that is what they did in those days', and you would be right. Very few of the Old Testament heroes had only one wife/partner. King Solomon had seven hundred wives, which I think is just ridiculous. As my husband would say, 'What man wants to be nagged by seven hundred women! He would never get any peace!'

Whether it was the done thing or not in those days, it was never God's will for that to happen, and he never approved of men taking more than one wife.

In the very first book of the Bible, Genesis, you can read in chapter 2:24:

> ...a man will leave his father and mother and be united to his wife, and they will become one flesh.

One man with one woman, singular not plural! God never condoned sexual relations with many partners—and he never will—but even the great heroes of the Bible were human and sinned. The only person who never sinned is Jesus. He is the one to look to for the perfect example.

Message for today

Sex is a subject I am sure you are all familiar with by now. You know that the pressure to have sex starts very early, and some of your non-Christian friends may already have been experimenting by now. It was hard to stand firm when I was at school, so I can only imagine how hard it is for you these days. When you are strongly attracted to someone and your friends are encouraging you, it can be very, very hard to resist. This is one essential reason why it is so important to date someone who is also a Christian and has the same beliefs as you.

God's plan for your life is for you to remain a virgin (i.e., never having sex) until your wedding night, and then to only be intimate with your husband or wife. If we love God truly and want to obey him, then, no matter what others have done or are doing, including the people we look up to, this is the way we should go.

Now, I hear you saying, 'Yes, but it's all right for you—you are married …', and you would be right. It is easy for me to say this now, but I didn't get married until I was thirty-four years old, so I have some idea of how hard it is, believe me. But I can also tell you that it was worth the wait!

So where does Esther fit into all this? (verses 5–8)

Well, Esther was one of the girls taken to the palace as potential queen material for Xerxes.

In this passage we read that Esther's real Hebrew name was Hadassah (verse 7). She became known as Esther to fit in with the area where she was now living. Her family were Jews, originating from the time when Nebuchadnezzar had overthrown the Jewish king Jehoiachin a few generations back and sent the Jews into exile.

The name Esther means 'star', and she really was a star! She was absolutely beautiful, but not just in looks. She had not had an easy life, as both her parents had died and her older cousin Mordecai had been bringing her up. However, there was no sign of her feeling sorry for herself; her personality was as stunning as her looks.

We are not told if she was taken to the palace by force or was quite happy to go. My hunch is that she was 'encouraged strongly' and went quietly.

A whole new world! (verses 9–12)

It must have been scary for her. She was brought into this huge palace with hundreds of other young girls, knowing that she was there to 'impress' one of the most powerful men in the known world. She would also have known that, once admitted to the harem, few women if any were ever allowed to leave.

It was going to be a full year before she even got to see the king for her one night (verse 12). She was to have six months of treatment with oil of myrrh, which was supposed to lighten the skin and make the girls more attractive, and then six months of perfumes and cosmetics.

And the problem with that?

If you, like me, are a girl who likes to be pampered, this suddenly doesn't sound too bad. Not so sure about wanting paler skin, as I love it when I get a tan, but the cosmetics and perfumes side sounds great ... and for twelve months! It sounds like a twelve-month spar treatment!

But remember, Esther was very unlikely to have had many, if any, friends there. Whatever methods were used to bring these girls into the palace, they would have known that they were stuck there now, but there could be worse ways to spend your days than as the queen. I imagine the competition would have been huge and very stressful.

So, imagine hundreds of girls all in one place, all vying for the Number 1 spot. I don't imagine the atmosphere would have been at all pleasant, but Esther had no choice.

And yet God was working his purpose out

There is a verse in Romans that really applies to this story. It is found in chapter 8 verse 28:

And we know that in all things God works for the good of those who love him, who have been called according to his purpose.

Esther must have felt at times that God had completely abandoned her, and I am sure most of us would have felt the same, but let us go through the story so far and the rest of chapter 2, and see the places where God was quietly working behind the scenes. Remember, any 'coincidence' is never a coincidence.

So far ...

• Vashti had been deposed.

• Esther's family had stayed in Susa and not gone back to their home country when they were given permission.

• Xerxes decided, upon advice, to hold a 'beauty pageant' to find his next queen.

• Esther was beautiful in looks and personality and was single—she was a winner.

• Esther was chosen as one of the potential candidates.

God's direction continues ... (verses 9–18)

• The chief in charge of the harem, Hegai, took an immediate liking to Esther and gave her special privileges, including the best quarters and her own maids (verse 9). This man had seen hundreds of beautiful girls come into his care— he would not have been easily impressed—and yet he just happened to be easily impressed with Esther.

• Esther had never revealed that she was a Jew, on the instructions of her cousin Mordecai (verse 10). Later we will see just why that was so vital.

• Every girl was allowed to bring one thing of

her choosing to the king when it was her night. Esther asked advice from Hegai about what it would be best to bring and she followed his suggestion (verse 15)—clever girl! We are not told what that suggestion was, but it clearly did not hurt ...

• After all the gorgeous women Xerxes must have seen, he just happened to fall head over heels in love with our girl after one night—enough to declare her queen then and there (verse 17).

All just coincidences, or God's direction? This story is too good to be true unless there was some divine intervention here. A young orphaned Jewish girl had become queen of the Persian Empire! Wow!

But the story doesn't end there ... really it had only just begun. God's plan wasn't just for Esther to become queen. Once queen, she had a huge calling to fulfil. She was going to save the Jewish people. That was the real plan—all this was just for starters.

Think tank

1. Esther wasn't the only character in the Bible who was led by God into situations he or she didn't quite understand the reason for. Can you think of any others? One was the subject of one of my other books.

For some ideas, read:

• Daniel chapter 6

• Genesis chapter 37 and chapters 39–41.

Describe briefly what happened to the characters in these chapters and why it had to happen. What was God's end result?

2. Do you have any idea why Mordecai would have advised Esther to keep her nationality a secret at this stage?

3. If you are at the age when sex is becoming a big issue, try to find a book on the subject written from a Christian perspective. It is vital you know what God says on this issue in the Bible, so that you can fully obey him. I know that it is difficult to make a stand in this area, especially when your body is telling you it would really rather do something completely different from what the Bible is saying. Pray hard that when you are tempted, you will be able to resist.

Note: If you do fail, or have failed, in this area and are truly sorry, do not think that this sin is unforgivable. That is not the case. God is ready to forgive any sin, no matter what it is, if we are truly sorry and strive not to repeat it.

White board.

'... "coincidence" means incidents that are a combination of God's guidance and a person's obedience.'

4. Mordecai: The unsung hero

Read Esther 2:19–23

This part of chapter 2 does not seem to follow the beginning of the chapter very well and seems quite out of place. One minute we are celebrating Esther's coronation as queen, and the next we are with her cousin at the king's gate.

However, this section will prove to be vitally important later in the book, so let's study it now and keep it in mind for later on.

Mordecai at the king's gate *(verses 19–20)*

Why the virgins were assembled for the second time when Xerxes had fallen in love with Esther, I do not know and am not sure I want to know. I don't think he was choosing another queen, but I think we will leave the question unanswered. Anyway, Mordecai was now sitting at the king's gate.

The king's gate was the official place where people in office sat. It would have been similar to today's law courts, a place where issues were raised and decisions made by people in authority. For Mordecai to be sitting there indicates that he was in a position of authority, which

would also explain how he could easily get messages through to Esther, and vice versa, while she was in the palace.

How handy that Mordecai was in such a position and therefore still had contact with Esther!

We are also again reminded in verse 20 that Esther had obeyed Mordecai and not revealed her Jewish heritage. Her allegiance was still very much towards Mordecai, and it would be tested to the limit later.

A plot uncovered (verses 21–22)

This position of authority also enabled Mordecai to find out about the plot to kill the king. Again, we are not told why these two officers had such a grudge against the king that they wanted him dead. Perhaps they were offered a sum of money by one of his enemies, or maybe it was because of a simple disagreement over wages—who knows. Either way, they were definitely not fighting the king's corner right now! How fortunate for the king that Mordecai was able to get word to Esther and the two officers were arrested before any damage could be done!

The investigations prove the plot to be true
(verse 23)

The legal process in Persia was not very different from our processes today, in that any charges brought against a person were always investigated first before the person was convicted. When Esther told the king about the plot Mordecai had uncovered, Xerxes did not simply take Esther's word for it.

Have you ever listened to some news (or gossip) and immediately believed it without checking out the facts?

For example: Some people love reading the gossip magazines for stories on celebrities' lives and what they are getting up to. I know it is not helpful reading, but people find it interesting all the same. I don't know how many times there are reports that a certain celebrity marriage is on the rocks. On the front cover the next week, though, is a headline about how in love the couple still are, and how they are planning to have a baby! Clearly the writers of these magazines don't do an awful lot of investigating. They hear a rumour and just run with the story without checking their facts. And readers fall for it each time.

Message for today

Think about your friends at school. How many times do you hear rumours about people in your class and can't help but spread those rumours? Do you ever stop to find out first whether or not they are true? That

is what we should do. Gossip is very mean and can be very hurtful, especially if a rumour is completely untrue. The next time you hear some gossip, try not to spread the news to anyone else. Keep your mouth shut and try to get the facts first, just as Xerxes did. Don't be the cause of making someone's life unfairly miserable.

These two officers were found guilty, though, and their punishment was the death sentence.

Points of 'coincidence'

As we go through this small passage, we can see that there are still a number of incidents that some would call 'coincidence' and I would call 'God's guiding'!

• Mordecai was in a position of authority and happened to be in the right place at the right time to uncover this plot.

• Mordecai's position of authority also enabled him to get messages to Esther really quickly.

• Mordecai was not immediately rewarded for saving the king's life, which in those times was very, very unusual.

In the next chapter, we finally meet the man Esther would have to come up against in the near future, and things hot up considerably. In the meantime, look through the list below and try to remember these points. It will be really helpful at a later stage.

Points to remember

• Esther still hadn't revealed her Jewish roots.

• Mordecai had not yet received a reward for uncovering the plot. There was a reason for that, as we shall find out later.

• This episode was written down in the records kept at the palace, including the fact that Mordecai was the person responsible for uncovering the plot. It would also have been recorded that no reward was given.

Think tank

1. In this chapter we have looked at points of 'coincidence', and the Bible is littered with 'coincidences'. Remember, as far as Christians are concerned, the word 'coincidence' means incidents that are a combination of God's guidance and a person's obedience.

Can you think of any other examples in the Bible of divine coincidence? I thought of two:

Joseph was promoted to governing the whole of Egypt because he told Pharaoh the meaning of his dream and warned of a famine. He was in charge of making provisions in readiness for the famine. The coincidence was that Joseph's family suffered in the famine and had to come all the way from Israel to Egypt, as the only spare food was stored there, thanks to Joseph. Joseph's brothers had to ask him, the one they had sold into slavery years before, to give them food. Of course, it was God's guidance all along. (See Genesis 41:41 to chapter 42.)

Joshua sent two spies into Jericho to look over the land before they invaded. The coincidence is that they happened to find a woman there called Rahab, who was happy to have them stay and help them to escape rather than hand them over to the king of Jericho. To find a woman who was willing to help people who were planning to invade her city would have been very rare. (See Joshua chapter 2).

2. Can you think of any episodes of 'coincidence' in your own life that now, looking back, you can see that God was guiding?

For example: A good friend of mine suddenly lost her mother in a horrible accident. She phoned me on the night it happened, which was a Friday. Her boyfriend was away on business and she was pretty much alone. The coincidence was that I had booked some annual leave for the following week. I had not booked a holiday but was planning to stay at home. This meant that I could get in the car and go to her and be there for the whole of the following week, seeing her through the funeral. God was clearly at work in this situation.

When a coincidence occurs in your life, remember, it means that God is guiding every area of your life.

'...The abilities you have are God-given and he deserves all the praise.'

5. *The trouble begins*

Read Esther 3:1–7

If this was a pantomime, you would have the audience booing right now as Haman enters the stage. However, Haman was not like the naughty but amusingly evil characters you find in the theatre. He was not a man to be messed with, and he was evil through and through. We are told nothing pleasant about him at all.

And yet, for some bizarre, unknown reason, Xerxes took a liking to him and elevated him to the role similar to that of a prime minister today (verse 1). I suspect he was promoted because he was the best at sucking up to the king and inflating the king's ego. In turn, the king decided on a course of action that would inflate Haman's ego too! And it worked. I can imagine how much Haman loved people bowing down to him. It made him feel so important.

At first, Haman clearly did not realize that Mordecai was the only one who refused to bow down to him (verse 2). There would have been so many people at the king's gate that Mordecai's actions could quite easily have been unnoticed in the crowd, until the other officials noticed it and brought it to Haman's attention (verse 3).

Why no bowing?

Again, we are not told exactly why Mordecai refused to

bow down to Haman. After all, if we met the Queen of England, I doubt many of us would have a problem bowing to her, even if we didn't particularly like her. Below are two suggestions that seem to make the most  sense to me. Keep in mind that Mordecai had been very open with these officials and had told them that he was a Jew (verse 4).

They had a history ... Let's have a history lesson!

Back in the past, Moses said that God would be at war with the Amalekites from generation to generation (look up Exodus 17:16). If you look at how Haman is introduced at the beginning of this chapter, it clearly states that he was an Agagite, otherwise known as an Amalekite. The term 'Agagite' is a reference to an old Amalekite king, Agag.

Moving on to 1 Samuel 15, we read about Saul (who happened to be an ancestor of Mordecai). He was Israel's first king and was commanded by God to wipe out the Amalekite race—for good reason, I assure you. But Saul disobeyed and spared King Agag. That had disastrous results not only for Saul, as in the future it would be an Amalekite who claimed that he had killed him, but also for Mordecai and Esther, as a direct descendant of Agag was about to give the Jewish race another run for their money.

Not deserved

Basically, Mordecai and Haman were destined not to get on, but I don't think that was Mordecai's reason for not bowing down. I suspect that he was not one to bear a grudge, unlike Haman. I honestly feel that it was simply a case of Haman not having earned his position and therefore Mordecai's respect. It probably went a bit further, in that Haman was almost demanding worship from those below him, and Mordecai would only worship God, not man!

Haman's reaction goes way too far *(verses 5–6))*

It doesn't take a genius to realize that Haman would have been none too pleased at finding out that Mordecai had not bowed down to him, but I suspect that his reaction would not have been quite so severe and out of proportion if Mordecai had belonged to another race. However, for Haman, this would be his time for revenge. He wanted not only Mordecai murdered, but the whole of the Jewish race with him.

Pride is a terrible problem that we all suffer with, and yet none of us deserves to be proud.

Message for today

Never elevate yourself above where you deserve to be. If you are given a position of head boy or girl or team captain, don't start thinking that you are more important than any other boy, girl, or member of the team. The abilities you have are God-given and he deserves all the praise. If you don't get the recognition you thought you deserved, swallow your pride and move on. Don't get illusions of grandeur, but be humble, thanking God for the gifts and abilities you have to help others.

An evil plan is devised! (verse 7)

The events from verse 7 onwards occurred approximately five years after Esther had become queen, which meant that Haman had had a fair amount of time to devise a way of getting rid of the Jews.

Verse 7 tells us a lot about where Haman's faith lay—in chance. The process of casting lots is mentioned quite a lot in the Bible as a way of choosing the right thing or person. It was used occasionally by Christians to make choices, their prayer being that the one chosen by lot would be the one God approved or disapproved of. It is not a recommended way of making decisions in churches today, mainly, I believe, because we now have the Bible and the help of the Holy Spirit to guide us, and that is all we need.

Generally, however, casting lots was used by those who followed false gods or believed in astrology, fortune-telling and witchcraft, and this was the case with Haman. So why was he wanting lots to be cast for a specific date? A date for what? Well, we soon find out that it was to choose a date for the annihilation of the Jewish race!

What does it mean to cast lots?

To cast lots, generally you would have a bag or a pot, and dice or stones would be placed in it, each one with a different marking to signify a specific decision or, as in Haman's case, a date. Usually a few incantations or spells would be spoken over the pot before one stone was removed, revealing the date or decision. Haman's idea was that whichever date was chosen would be a 'lucky' day, meaning that his plan would be successful!

Content:

Message for today

The casting of lots may all sound a little silly and basic to us, but even today people believe in luck and chance and think that their destiny is ruled by the date they were born or where the sun, moon and stars are placed at a certain time.

How many of you read the horoscopes in magazines or newspapers? Mostly, I know, it is just for a laugh, but be careful. It is surprisingly easy to get sucked into this kind of thing, and before you know it, you are reading horoscopes before you make any decisions. Think about it logically. Why would you look to the stars for guidance when we have the gift of being able to look to the Creator of these stars for guidance instead?

I had a friend at school who started to read the horoscopes 'for a laugh' and then got addicted to reading them, started visiting fortune-tellers, and ended up in quite a state, with serious nightmares and difficulty sleeping. When I was helping to lead a youth group, playing with a Ouija board was quite popular among teenagers. Please, please, don't get involved. My advice would be not to touch these things with a barge-pole. The occult and evil spirits are very real and are totally against God. They are not something to be taken lightly or to be made a joke out of! Satan is no cute and cuddly man in red with small horns and a cheeky grin. He is real and he means business. He will lure people away from God at any and every opportunity, and he

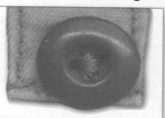

just loves it when young people start reading horoscopes, believing in chance/luck, and dabbling in the occult, whether or not it is only meant to be 'for a laugh'!

OK, lecture over—let's get back to the passage in the next chapter.

Think tank

1. Can you think of other episodes in the Bible where lots were cast to make decisions? Look up these passages if you need help:

- Jonah chapter 1
- John 19:23–24
- Acts 1:15–26.

2. There are at least two episodes in the Bible where Satan tries to lure people away from God. Look up:

- Job chapter 1. Satan was trying to ruin Job's faith in God by bringing about all sorts of catastrophes.

- Luke 4:1–13. Satan was trying to tempt Jesus not to complete his mission. If he had succeeded, we would have no way of getting to heaven, and Satan knew that!

Satan doesn't seem quite so cute and cuddly now, does he?

3. Have a discussion with your friends about fairground fortune-telling or reading horoscopes. Do you agree with me about the seriousness of these things? You need to make up your own mind about this issue, but ask for God to guide you in this area.

' . . . Each one of us—no matter what colour our skin, language we speak or culture we follow—is part of God's creation. '

6. The trouble continues

Read Esther 3:8–4:3

Xerxes agrees to Haman's evil plan! *(3:8–10)*

Haman may have been a despicable character but he was very cunning and clever.

Look at his speech to Xerxes in verse 8 and you will notice how vague his petition was.

- He never mentioned which people he had a problem with, using the phrase 'a certain people'.
- He did not mention why the different customs would have been a problem for Xerxes.
- He did not mention which of the king's laws these people did not obey.
- He did not say why it was not in the king's best interests to 'tolerate' these people.

Remember, neither Xerxes nor Haman knew that Esther was a Jew, but maybe Haman was worried that Xerxes had close advisors who were Jews and he did not want to risk Xerxes turning against him. Haman also knew that he didn't really have a case at all and that he had little evidence that the Jews were causing Xerxes any problem whatsoever. He was taking a big risk, giving Xerxes such little information about the group of people that Haman wanted eradicated.

Note: Take a moment to think about what Haman was asking of Xerxes. He was not wanting something small. It was not a case of simply

charging the Jews more taxes than others, or ensuring they bought the king a bigger birthday present! Haman wanted all the Jewish people destroyed! He wanted every Jew to be killed on that day—including young, old, women and children—and all their possessions to be taken. It was not a request to be taken lightly, and yet that is exactly how Xerxes seemed to react to it.

Xerxes readily agreed without asking any questions at all. He gave the impression that life was cheap and he did not care one way or the other. It did not matter who these people were—they were nothing to him. If Haman said that they were a problem and they were different, then that was so; let him do what he wanted with them. This was a dangerous man to have as a king.

Message for today

Haman had a grudge against one person, decided that the whole of that person's race must be bad, and so wanted them all to be destroyed.

Xerxes took the word of one man who said that one group of people were 'different', so had no problem with ordering their destruction.

What about you?

How do you treat people who are from a different culture or race? Whether you agree with their customs or not, or find them a little unusual, remember, they probably find your culture unusual too. Each one of us—

no matter what colour our skin, language we speak or culture we follow—is part of God's creation. He made each and every one of us, and we should therefore love each other, without judgement, as God loves us and gave his own Son to die for us. How can we expect to be good examples of our faith to other people if we do not show them love?

Hopefully, none of us bears such a grudge that we would want to follow the same route as Haman (although you do often hear of regular fights between gangs of different races in cities throughout the world), but we can still all be guilty of some form of prejudice.

For example (1): I remember that, when I was at school, there was a girl in my class who was a Muslim. She covered her hair and always wore trousers under her skirt to hide her legs. This is the Muslim custom when girls get to a certain age. I believe the idea is to prevent men who are not their husbands looking at them in a sexual way. I also recall that this girl got teased a lot because of how she dressed, yet I remember her as being a lovely girl.

I am sure that you can think of someone in your class at school who also gets teased for his or her culture or customs. Please don't get drawn into that kind of behaviour.

For example (2): The awful terrorist attack on the World Trade Center in New York in 2001 left a lot of people feeling very angry towards all Muslims, not just towards the evil organizations that carried out the attack. Many Muslims will say how they have been badly treated because they belong to the same faith as those terrorists.

Don't be like Haman and believe that one bad egg spoils the whole batch (although Haman was not even right to think that Mordecai was a 'bad egg' anyway). If you look back into Christian history you will discover many times, especially during the Crusades, when people did awful things to others in the name of Christianity. Every culture has episodes in its history that its people are ashamed of, but we shouldn't write off the whole race or culture because of a group of people who were very wrong.

The evil plan is sealed with the king's ring
(3:10–15)

So, not only was the king casually happy to agree to Haman's wish for a mass genocide on a people whose identity he did not know, but he was also willing to seal the order with his own ring. This meant that no one, not even the king himself, could reverse the order. It might as well have been written in stone.

Note: He also refused the offer of payment from Haman for agreeing to his plan, but historians know that this was the custom when money was first offered for a favour. To offer to pay was the polite thing to do but was rarely meant. Haman would probably have planned to pay from the looting of the Jews' property—and he did pay, but not quite in the way he had imagined!

So the order went out by the Persian express postal service, and everyone would have known what was being ordered for that awful day. I am always amazed that there is no mention of the Jews making a run for the border. I know I would definitely head for the hills if I was pre-warned that someone would be coming to kill me on a certain day in the future. Maybe they had nowhere else to go, or maybe they had faith that God would somehow rescue them. Maybe some of them did emigrate. All we are told is that, while Haman and Xerxes were happily

drinking away, the town of Susa was rocked by the news (verse 15).

This epic chapter ends with the horrible image of two men of power having sent out an order to eradicate a whole race, then sitting together without a care in the world. Thankfully, the story doesn't end here!

All a bit depressing! (4:1–3)

So things were all looking rather depressing. It seemed to be an impossible situation, especially with the king having sealed the petition with his own ring so that no one could revoke it. Remember, though, that nothing is impossible and that God is always working away, even if it seems he is very much in the background, as in the book of Esther.

Mordecai, Esther's cousin, would have heard about the command early on, especially given his position near the king's gate. He immediately dressed in sackcloth and ashes and went out into the city, wailing loudly.

Why the bizarre dress code?

You can understand Mordecai and all the Jews being pretty depressed about the order, and as you probably know, in Eastern society it is quite common for there to be public wailing and weeping during a bad time. On the TV you might have seen pictures of funerals held in Eastern countries, particularly given all the terrorist attacks between Israel and Palestine. The mourners are quite vocal in their mourning. But you have probably never  seen anyone wearing sackcloth and ashes before.

This was another sign of mourning that was quite common in biblical times. King David was known to have worn this apparel when the occasion warranted, and the people of Nineveh were ordered to dress in this way when they heard from Jonah about God's judgement on them for their evil ways (look up Jonah 3:7–9).

Sackcloth: An old material that was traditionally made from goat's hair and was very rough and itchy to wear—not a pleasant material. When I was a girl, we used to put potatoes into sackcloth after harvesting them on my uncle's farm.

Ashes: These were literally ashes from a burnt fire that mourners would put on their heads.

People would be under no illusions that the person

wearing this outfit was not a happy camper!

Note: Until recently, people always tended to wear black to a funeral in the Western world as a sign of mourning, but that tradition seems to be disappearing a little now.

Clearly the news of his nation's upcoming annihilation would be enough for anyone to think Mordecai's dress code of mourning, along with his behaviour outside the king's gate, was appropriate, but I think there was another reason for his obvious display of distress. As we have already seen, Mordecai did have a link with Esther through the guards and servants at the gate. He clearly realized the Jews' only hope would be through Esther and her position in the palace, and he needed to get the message of what was going on through to her. By carrying on as he did, it would get the guards' attention, and hopefully they would relay the information to Esther that her cousin was in distress.

And this was exactly what happened ...

Think tank

1. Haman stated that one of the reasons for his petition was because these 'certain people' had different customs. They stood out.

Do we stand out for being different? If you are a Christian, do your friends at school know this and what you stand for, or do you hide in the crowd and not say anything when the subject comes up? Think about it. It is good to be different and stand out for God. Try not to be embarrassed about your faith but be open about how much Christ means to you. I know it is not easy, and I struggle with it too, but we should never lower our standards just to blend in.

2. Think of examples of how you can stand out as a Christian at school or among friends and family.

3. There are many situations in the Bible where things looked impossible but God made the impossible possible. Try to think of some yourself. Here are just two I thought of:

- Acts 16:16–34—Paul and Silas had a miraculous experience in prison.
- Genesis 18:1–15; 21:1–3—Sarah, Abraham's wife, had a child in old age.

'. . . God is always there and is all-powerful.'

7. Esther takes centre stage

Read Esther 4:4–17

Esther was clueless *(verse 4)*

OK, so the whole of her race was due to face annihilation in the near future so Esther, having heard about Mordecai's state of serious mourning, sent her maids with proper clothes for him, in an attempt to cheer him up. Quite a bizarre reaction, really—a new outfit would really make everything better!

For example: As far as the English are concerned, a cup of tea will solve everything and anything. Someone's relative has just died and the friend's first comment is, 'Let's have a cup of tea'. Someone loses a job and immediately the kettle goes on. If Esther had been English, I am sure that she would have sent out a hot cuppa rather than a new set of clothes.

Anyway, we soon discover that her reaction was actually not that bizarre at all, as she had no idea what was going on. Generally speaking, it was against the law to be in the king's presence and be miserable. Everyone had to be happy, otherwise they might make the king unhappy, and that would never do. To ensure that the important people (like the queen) stayed happy, the officials never informed them what was going on outside the palace. Today, they would have been prevented from watching TV or reading newspapers, but in those days they were simply not allowed to have any contact with the outside world. So Esther had no knowledge of the new order at all.

Esther gets a shock and a very difficult request from her cousin (verses 5–11)

When Mordecai refused her offer of clothes, she sent out a personal servant, Hathach, who found out the problem. Clearly, Mordecai felt the need to back up his story with proof, so he sent the servant back with a copy of the order so that Esther would be in no doubt that it was all real.

Did he think Esther would not believe him?

I don't think that was the case, but Mordecai knew that he was about to ask something very difficult of her that would require a lot of courage, and it was therefore important that she fully understood the situation. He did not want his message to get lost in translation.

The request: Go to the king and beg for mercy and plead for the Jewish people.

Why was this such a difficult request?

It is hard to imagine it today. Recently, I asked my husband if we could have satellite TV as, being in South Africa, I really miss my English programmes, and the satellite channels include the BBC channels. This is a small request compared with the one Esther had to make, and I wasn't worried about Stuart's reaction, or anxious that he would ban me from his presence or look for a new wife because I was being cheeky. I definitely wasn't worried that he would order the death penalty for my coming to him uninvited! And yet that was exactly the case in Esther's day. Not even a queen could enter the king's presence unless he had called her, and if he had called her, and if  she did appear uninvited and he was not happy about it (demonstrated by his not extending his golden sceptre), she would be put to death.

How scary is that! Some people have criticized Esther's initial response to Mordecai's request (verse 11), but I can understand it. She was still a young woman and was scared of the king. She knew the rules, and I think anyone would have to admit that the thought of potentially being put to death is not a happy one.

There was one more thing …

Esther had not been invited into the king's presence for thirty days. She might have been concerned that she was losing her appeal or had one something to offend him the last time she was with him. If that was the case, he would not take too kindly to being interrupted by her in his court.

Message for today

Esther's reluctance and timidity are completely understandable in this situation, but how often we are reluctant or timid when confronted with situations that are nowhere near as difficult as Esther's and with not nearly such dire consequences!

When I was in my late teens/early twenties, a group from my church used to go to the town centre of Kingston-upon-Thames, near London, with an old double-decker bus, and talk about Christ to teenagers who were hanging around the streets late at night. I will be honest: it scared the life out of me. I knew it was what God wanted me to do, but every week I hoped that I would have to do a late shift and work on a Friday and so be unable to attend.

I don't believe it is wrong to be scared, as that is a natural reaction to the thought of being ridiculed and teased. But at the same time, it was wrong for me to look for excuses and for a way out. Instead, I should have been praying more often that God would be with me and calm my nerves.

Esther really had no choice (verses 12–14)

Mordecai's reply to Esther was firm but fair. At the end of the day, Esther was a Jew, and Mordecai knew she would not be singled out for special treatment on that awful day but would be killed along with the rest of them.

Her choice really boiled down to:

• Go to the king and risk being put to death, but potentially save her people.

• Do nothing and face certain death along with her people.

When Mordecai put it like that, it was obvious that Esther had no option, but when we look at his full reply we see that Mordecai clearly had a huge amount of faith in God (see verse 14). He trusted that God's purpose would be worked out whether Esther obeyed or not. He believed that God would not let his people perish and that his will would be done. If Esther refused, then God would just find some other way for his purpose to be carried out, but Esther and her family would suffer.

If Mordecai had been around during New Testament times, I think he would have quoted Paul from Romans 8:28:

And we know that in all things God works for the good of those who love him, who have been called according to his purpose.

Mordecai's speech was as good as any political campaign speech I have ever heard, and he ended it with something that would really have hit Esther hard.

Again, although God's name isn't mentioned, it is clearly implied that Mordecai believed that Esther's becoming queen had been God's plan all along so that she would be in a good position to help her people when the time came—and the time was now! Mordecai clearly didn't believe in coincidence either, but fully believed that everything happened for a reason.

Message for today

There will be many times in your life when certain things will happen and initially you will not be able to understand why.

Mordecai's message hits home *(verses 15–17)*

The motivational speech clearly worked and hit a chord with Esther. It is clear that her faith was strong too, as her first request was for her people to pray and fast for her. She too would pray and fast for three days.

Yes, I know it only says 'fast' in the Bible, but the whole point of fasting (i.e. not eating or drinking) was, and still is, to spend time praying to God and not get distracted by trivial things, such as preparing food. When people fast, it shows that they are truly earnest in the cause they are praying for, to the point of coping with hunger and thirst so that they can dedicate the time to God and prayer.

Message for today

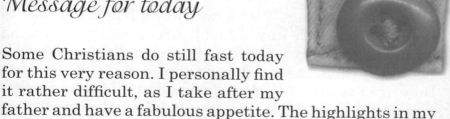

Some Christians do still fast today for this very reason. I personally find it rather difficult, as I take after my father and have a fabulous appetite. The highlights in my day often involve eating! I have tried fasting but I found that my mind was wandering to food rather than to God, and my stomach rumbles were louder than the prayers. However, I think that says more about the failings in my

spiritual life than about the merits of fasting. If you are a Christian, it is not a rule that you have to fast, but some people find it really helpful, and fasting definitely shows that they are earnestly seeking God's help in a certain matter. Obviously, three days of not eating and drinking was a huge commitment for Esther and the Jews, but then they were all facing death anyway. Whether you decide to fast or not, the prayer part is always essential for everything in life, especially before a major event or when faced with illness or a problem we have to deal with. How can we expect God to help us through difficult times if we never earnestly ask him to intervene, assist or comfort?

For example: I can remember, as a young child, rushing up to my parents if I had any problem at school and telling them all about it. As a child, you often think that your parents have all the answers, and even just talking about a problem to them would make you feel better. Good parents love nothing more than for their children to come and talk to them about their problems. It is the same with God, apart from one subtle but very important difference: God can intervene and he has the power to help you through any difficult areas you are dealing with. His wisdom is perfect. Occasionally, parents are not able to help their children through difficult times, as they are not always able to be present and they are not perfect. But God is always there and is all-powerful, as Esther found out.

Once the three days of fasting were complete, Esther said, she would go to the king and risk her life in the process. It comes across as if she had fully accepted that she had to do this, and was resigned to leaving it in God's hands. As she said,

If I perish, I perish.

I think this was so brave of her, and I just hope that, if I was ever in a life-threatening situation like hers, I would have the courage to do the right thing too.

So we end this section on a bit of a cliffhanger. Will the king listen to Esther, or will Haman get his way? To be continued ...

Think tank

1. Name some other people, preferably in the Bible, who were reluctant and scared when first given a mission by God. For ideas read:
   - Jonah 1:1–3
   - Exodus 4:1–17
   - Acts 9:1–15
   - Luke 22:39–46.

2. Are you going through a hard time right now and cannot see God's hand at work at all? I promise you that he's there. You may not know the reason for the trials you face in this life, but there is one, and you will definitely find out in heaven.

4. When you are in trouble, do you automatically go to God as Esther did, or is he a last resort when nothing else has worked?

'... so when you are faced with a decision, listen to him.'

8. Esther shows what she is truly made of

Read Esther 5:1–8

On the last day of fasting Esther made her move. Like all wise wives who are asking a favour from their husbands, she dressed up to look as lovely as possible and put on royal robes that the king himself would have given her. Granted, this task was a little more important than the average request from most wives, who, if they are anything like me, usually centre those requests around some new clothes or a holiday—but you get the idea.

Now we see how God really answers prayer in ways that can take everyone by surprise.

God gives Esther wisdom to deal with the situation *(verses 1–6)*

Esther did not go in with all guns blazing, blurting out who she really was and demanding that something be done about this horrible order to annihilate her race. Look at verses 1–4.

Esther positioned herself in the inner court, where she was likely to be seen at some point by the king, but where she would not appear too intrusive, interrupting a present discussion—*very wise.*

She did not say a word. Once the king saw her—and, thankfully, he was pleased to see her—she simply and humbly approached and touched the tip of the sceptre, as was their custom—*very wise*.

She waited until she was spoken to by the king before she made any move—*very wise*.

Her language was very submissive and humble (I imagine there are many husbands who would not mind their wives speaking to them in more gentle, submissive tones than they usually do—including my own husband at times)—*very wise*.

She invited the king and Haman to an intimate banquet/meal, before bringing her request to him (any wife worth her salt knows that the way to a man's heart is often through his stomach, and a good meal can work wonders)—*very wise*.

But why invite Haman?

Perhaps you are thinking that it wasn't wise at all to be inviting the Jews' sworn enemy. Why would Esther want him there when she had something to say against him?

There is a saying that goes, 'Keep your friends close but your enemies even closer'. I think that is rather appropriate for this point in the story. Esther did not want Haman to get any ideas that she was up to something behind his back. His guard would be completely down, and he would have thought he was in the queen's favour and was very honoured to be invited to such a personal banquet. When we get further on in this chapter, you will see that that was exactly what Haman thought, and his pride went through the roof!

So where did Esther get all this amazing wisdom from?

It is not stated in the book, but I think it is clear that God was working in an amazing way. Note that God was not only working in Esther.

King Xerxes was, I suspect, *unusually* happy to see Esther, and he waived the death order immediately by offering her his sceptre (verse 2). He was also unusually generous in how he spoke to her.

Haman did not detect a hint of a problem with Esther's request and was not at all suspicious of her.

One more interesting point

Just look again at how King Xerxes spoke to Esther in verses 3 and 6. In both verses he asked to know her request, and before he even heard it, said that it would be given to her, even offering up to half his kingdom. This was a very frivolous, throw-away comment that I am sure the king did not really mean. I think he would have been shocked if Esther really had asked for half his kingdom. However, it was also a very stupid thing to say. Thankfully for Xerxes, he said this comment to a trustworthy girl who would never take advantage.

Message for today

I have heard many people say things like, 'I would do anything to have a new car', or 'Over my dead body will you go out with that boy or girl'. Do they really mean it? Would they really do absolutely anything to get what they wanted? What if that 'anything' included jumping off a cliff? Would someone really be prepared to die in order to stop another person going out with a girl or boy? Really?

From my own personal experience of using throw-away comments, I don't think so! In a year or two, there will be another car on the market these people would rather have and the old model will be forgotten. In a few months, they will have moved on from that person they would have 'died for' and will be concerned about someone else entirely. Be careful about the language you use and the phrases you use without thinking. You could come to regret it deeply.

Why the delay? *(verses 7–8)*

So, after the banquet, Esther had the floor. The men were fed and watered and feeling very accommodating. Again, the king asked what Esther wanted from him, and she had his full attention. To you or me, this would seem the ideal moment to tell him the whole story, ask him to save her people and punish Haman … but not for Esther. Instead, all she did was to invite both men to another banquet the next day and promise to answer the king then. So why the delay? It doesn't make sense to us, and it probably didn't make that much sense to Esther, but I believe that God knew the timing wasn't quite right. He had further work to do on Xerxes before he would be ready to listen to Esther, as we shall see in Esther chapter 6.

I believe Esther was guided in this and for some reason felt she had to wait until the following day.

For example: My brother married a girl who happened to be a good friend of mine, which worked out beautifully for me. When the two first met, they were both dating other people, but the time came when they were both unattached again. I was away at college at the time and kept getting phone calls from my brother, wondering whether this girl was interested in him. I also kept getting messages from my friend, sometimes through other friends, asking whether my brother was interested in her. Amazingly for me, I didn't get involved either way, but eventually, when my brother finally felt the time was right, he asked my friend out. A number of people had noticed the attraction between the two of them much earlier and wondered why they had taken so long, but my brother had to wait for just the right moment, and when that moment came, he knew and he conquered! Why didn't I get involved and speed things up? Again, I just felt that it would not have been right, and that, in my brother's good time, he would get round to it ... which he did! God does guide in this way, so when you are faced with a decision, listen to him and go with your convictions after praying about the matter first.

Note: One thing that surprises me is that Esther's reply about waiting till the next day was accepted by both men. She could easily have angered the king by her delay and have aroused suspicion

in Haman about what this was all about. I know that curiosity would definitely have got the better of me. By this point, I would have been quite frustrated, and Haman and Xerxes do not strike me as having been the most patient and laid-back of men! Another example of God working behind the scenes.

Think tank

1. There is one king in the New Testament who made the same offer given by Xerxes (offering up to half his kingdom) and it led to disastrous consequences. Can you think who it was? Read Mark 6:21–28.

2. Do you ever make rash statements that you don't really mean? It could be something as simple as offering your friend 'anything you want' so long as you can play with his or her DS or iPod. Try to think before you speak, and make sure that you mean what you say.

3. Can you think of other characters in the Bible who showed extreme wisdom that was given by God? One obvious example can be found in 1 Kings 3:16–28.

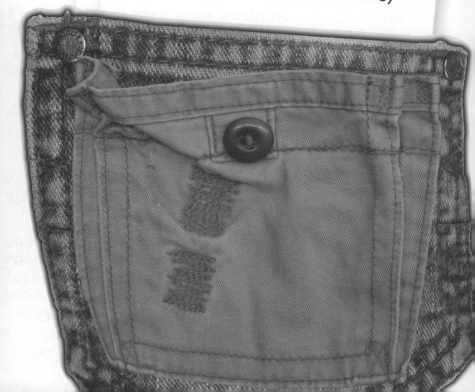

' . . . Love does not delight in evil but rejoices with the truth. '

(1 Corinthians 13 v 6)

9. *Pride comes before a fall*

Read Esther 5:9–14

Do you ever find yourself in a very good mood, when everything seems to be right with the world, and then one small negative thing happens and suddenly you are depressed? I know it happens to me.

It can be Friday evening and I have the following day to look forward to, a day filled with seeing friends or shopping or going travelling or shopping or going to the beach or shopping! Then one small thing can spoil my mood for the rest of the evening—and usually it is a very small thing. There might be a power cut, or my husband might be late back from work, and the way I react would make you think that I had just been told that all my wages were going to the tax man. As humans, our moods are very unpredictable, and this was the case with Haman.

There he was, as happy as could be and feeling very proud of himself.

He was chief advisor to the king and was incredibly powerful.

He had succeeded in forming a plan that would eradicate the Jews, and the king had bought the idea and signed the decree so that no one could change it.

Even the queen now clearly favoured him among all other nobles and had invited him to not one but two banquets.

I am sure that Haman thought things could not get any better ... until he passed Mordecai at the gate and again received no recognition for his status. Straight away this ruined Haman's good mood and sent him into a rage. He rushed home and immediately boasted to his wife and friends about how much he had and how honoured he was, but said that Mordecai sitting at the king's gate took all the satisfaction away (verses 11–13). How pathetic! Haman had been blessed beyond all imagination, and he let a little thing like one man not bowing to him—a man who, as far as Haman was concerned, was on death row anyway—to depress him and ruin it all.

Haman was a proud man, but also a very ungrateful one. He had a lot to be grateful for, but he was consumed by his hatred for this one man.

Message for today

I am sure that you struggle with mood swings too, especially if the hormones are starting to kick in.

For example: You have just come home for the summer holidays and the first thing your mum says to you as you walk through the door is that you now have time to tidy your room.

When I was a teenager, this would have been like a red rag to a bull for me, but it is important to try to get a little perspective here. Count to ten and try to remember all the reasons why you were in a good mood. You might have six to eight weeks off school. You might have an excellent family holiday planned or some great days out with your friends. You can sleep late every morning and stay up later at night. You have a comfortable bed to sleep in, and plenty of food and water. I could carry on the list of things to be grateful for, but you get the idea. All of a sudden, getting wound up over your mum's request seems a little pathetic, doesn't it? Tidying your room will really not make a huge impact on your free time, and your mum does do an awful lot for you without complaining. Taking some time out to think like this will hopefully stop your fast-approaching bad mood in its tracks, and you will be a better man or woman than Haman as a result.

It runs in the family

When you are having a problem or are just generally in a bad mood, it is always good to have someone to go to, who, as my father would say, has a good head on his or her shoulders. This person is understanding and good at listening, but also can see the other side of things and, if necessary, can tell you to stop being so silly and pick yourself up.

Haman, unfortunately, mixed with people who were as bad as he was and encouraged him in completely the wrong direction. His wife was the worst of all. I sometimes wonder whether she was even worse than Haman himself. She naturally assumed, as, clearly, did Haman and his friends, that the king would go along with whatever Haman wished. Clearly Mordecai deserved to die now, rather than wait for the mass annihilation later that year. She was so sure that Xerxes would agree that she advised Haman to build the gallows first in anticipation of the king's approval in the next day or so ... BIG MISTAKE!

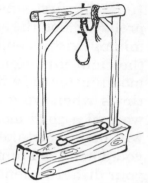

If I have learnt one thing in life, it is to never assume anything! This was to be the start of Haman's downfall.

Message for today

Haman mixed with the wrong crowd. It may seem as if his friends supported him, and he may have felt that they did too, but they were encouraging his wrong attitudes, probably for their own financial gain. They were not advising him to do what was right but what was evil, and those kinds of friends Haman did not need.

What about you? Look at your circle of close friends.

- When you are moaning about your parents or brothers/sisters/family, do your friends encourage you to moan even more, or bring you round and tell you that they are really not that bad?

- Do your friends encourage you to break rules

or keep them?

• Do they encourage you to lie to your parents and be difficult with them, or to try to be honest with them and get on well?

If the first answer in each case is true, they are probably not the greatest friends to have around. Try mixing with people who are going to encourage you in the right direction and tell it to you straight if you are moaning for the wrong reasons. We have all been through times when we didn't agree with our parents and just wanted a good moan, and no parent is perfect. Parents will make mistakes at times, but so will you. However, you don't need to moan to someone who is going to blow your disagreement all out of proportion.

It is the same principle when you start looking for a boyfriend or girlfriend. You want someone who is going to encourage you in your Christian faith and encourage you to attend youth group and church. You want someone who you can share your problems with and who will build you up and support you in the right way. And trust me, it is much easier if you find someone who actually gets on with your parents. Your parents won't give you nearly so much grief then.

So we leave Haman at the height of his pride and feeling as if he is on top of the world. What I find very interesting is the way verse 9 is phrased:

Haman went out that day happy and in high spirits.

The emphasis to me is on the words 'that day'. That day would be the last day he would ever be happy. Here comes the fall.

Think tank

1. Mood swings are a common problem. Don't feel too bad about them, as we all suffer with them at times, and you will be especially prone to them as you approach adulthood. It is not an easy time, and it is only when you have come through the other side that you realize they were a problem. Don't think your parents don't understand, either. They had to go through it too, and they struggled just as much as you do, and probably still do struggle at times. Ask God to help you to control your mood swings daily, and work at taking time out whenever you feel the anger rising.

2. What does the Bible say about a good wife? Read Proverbs 31:10–12, 30 and Ephesians 5:22–24.

What does the Bible say about a good husband? Read Ephesians 5:25–28. (In other words, boys, you must love your future wife so much that you would be prepared to die for her.)

What does the Bible say about love? Read 1 Corinthians 13:4–7.

These verses describe the type of partners we are to look for and how we ourselves are to be—something to think about when you are romantically interested in someone.

'... God's timing is always perfect.'

10. Ouch, that had to hurt!

Read Esther 6:1–14

Chapter 6 opens on the night after the first banquet, when the king cannot sleep. We are not given a specific reason for this, and it seems quite odd, considering that he would have eaten a huge meal and probably drunk a fair bit of wine. If my family is anything to go by, most men have no trouble sleeping after eating a big meal. (In fact, I have to admit that I, too, like a bit of shut-eye after my mother's Sunday roast dinner!) It must have been God at work, giving the king insomnia (inability to sleep). Look at this chain of events:

• The king had insomnia

—COINCIDENCE OR GOD AT WORK?

• He asked for the record of his reign to be brought out and read to him. This sounds a bit tedious—I imagine that the reader had a very monotonous voice. I reckon the king specifically asked for these records to be read so that they would send him to sleep, but it didn't work

—COINCIDENCE OR GOD AT WORK?

• Out of all the records, the reader chose to read from the part describing how Mordecai had exposed the plot to assassinate the king
—COINCIDENCE OR GOD AT WORK?

• Xerxes was actually paying attention, and I suspect may even have remembered the incident but not remembered giving any reward. Otherwise, why would he check to find out whether a reward had been given?

—COINCIDENCE OR GOD AT WORK?

• Just at the time when Xerxes realized that Mordecai had not been rewarded, who should walk in but Haman. Talk about wrong place at the wrong time

—COINCIDENCE OR GOD AT WORK?

If you have read my other books, you will no doubt have a strong suspicion that I definitely believe it was God at work, and you would be right. There was just too much that was out of the ordinary going on here. The amazing thing was that Xerxes was reminded of Mordecai's good work the very night before Haman had intended to ask permission to have Mordecai hanged.

Message for today

God's timing is always perfect. I know that often we get impatient and wonder why God is taking so long and doesn't seem to be at work in a particular area at all, but he knows much more than we do, and he will never act too early and NEVER act too late, even if sometimes it may seem that way to us.

For example: I was married at a fairly late age compared with most other Christian women in the UK, and I can remember that there were times when I wondered whether I would ever get married at all. There were many times when I saw my close friends getting married and I would get quite frustrated with God for not allowing me to meet Mr Right. I could not understand why he was making me wait so long. Would it ever happen at all? Now, looking back, I can see that God's timing in bringing Stuart along was perfect. I would not have been ready emotionally to cope with marriage until I was in my thirties. There was too much I had wanted to do, and I had not realized that along with marriage come sacrifice and compromise—things that I am still learning now. I also realize that being single in my twenties enabled me to devote more time to God and to church activities, such as the youth work and courses explaining the Christian faith. Now I am married, I realize that time is no longer mine to do exactly what I want with it. Don't get me wrong—I am loving married life!—but I now realize that God knew what he was doing in making me wait for it. His timing was perfect.

It now makes complete sense to realize that God guided Esther to wait another night before speaking to the king about her problem.

Haman gets completely the wrong idea!
(verses 4–10)

I doubt that Xerxes meant to be so vague about the identity of the man he wanted to honour, but Haman got completely carried away in his own self-importance. Xerxes simply asked Haman what he, as king, should do for the man he wanted to honour. There was no mention of it being a reward for a past deed, and no mention of who this man was that the king wanted to honour.

Having said that, it does reveal an awful lot of pride on Haman's part for him immediately to think that the king wanted to honour him. He thought he was so special to the king that he could not possibly be referring to anyone else, so he immediately went into an elaborate, over-the-top description of what should be done for this man. Clearly he fancied being paraded through the city in royal robes on the king's horse! What a fool! This would have inflated Haman's ego even further, if that were possible ...

But ...

Haman had one tiny little detail wrong. Xerxes had no plan to honour him at all; instead, he meant Mordecai, Haman's sworn enemy (verse 10).

I can't help but laugh at the thought of Haman's face when he heard Mordecai's name. His jaw must have hit the floor and his heart must have sunk far enough to meet his jaw on that floor! This could not have been any worse news, and I wonder if Haman already saw all his future plans start to unravel, even at this early stage. I imagine that it wasn't long before beads of perspiration started to form on his forehead.

Note: One interesting fact is that Xerxes specifically called Mordecai a Jew, but there appears to have been no recognition that the Jews were the very race he had agreed to annihilate in a few months' time. Xerxes clearly still had no idea which race Haman had in mind for the massacre.

It doesn't say much for Xerxes' character that he had apparently shown no interest in the decree he had agreed to so readily.

Haman did not have a leg to stand on, and he knew better than to contradict the king. He shut his mouth (probably for the first time in a long time) and went and did exactly as the king ordered.

The contrast (verses 11–12)

We are not told how Mordecai reacted when Haman found him and told him what was about to happen. I imagine that he praised God and saw this as a sign that God was working out his purpose. Perhaps he was also a little embarrassed by the whole affair.

What we are told is his reaction afterwards. Contrast it with Haman's reaction to being invited to two banquets by the queen:

- Haman was full of pride, and went home boasting about how important he was.

- Mordecai just went back to work very humbly at the king's gate. There is no mention of any boasting at all.

Quiz question: Which attitude is the best example for us? Not exactly rocket science, I know, but how many times do we want to boast about things that have happened to us?

For example: While I was district nursing, I looked after a very famous client. Now, it is against the rules to talk about anyone you are looking after outside work, so I had to keep quiet, but you have no idea how hard it was. Every time this person's name came up or I saw the person in a movie, I was desperate to share my story with friends and family—but why? Because I wanted to boast about it, and that was wrong. I wasn't more important because of this famous contact, and I had nothing to boast about.

As Paul says so well in 1 Corinthians 1:31,

Let him who boasts boast in the Lord.

Jesus Christ, and what he did for us in dying on the cross, is the only thing we can boast about, and that is not because of anything we have done but all because of what he did for us.

Message for today

When you are tempted to boast about something you did or something you have, stop! Remember, nothing we have is ours. Everything is a gift from God. As Haman was about to find out, these things can be taken away again just as easily as they were given. Be thankful and not proud.

Who needs enemies when you have a wife like Zeresh? (verses 12–14)

As soon as Haman had completed his task, he rushed home to tell his wife all the awful things that had happened. I imagine he was looking for some comfort and reassurance, but Zeresh doesn't strike me as the reassuring sort. In fact, she seemed to be able to make Haman feel ten times worse.

Again, we are not told that Zeresh was aware of Haman's plan for the Jewish race, but the decree was issued in the citadel in Susa and all the Jews had heard about it, so I think she would have needed to have had her head in the sand in order not to have heard about it, even if Haman had not told her. However, she saw this honouring of Mordecai as a sign that the writing was on the wall for Haman, for at least two possible reasons.

• I think she sensed that Xerxes would never allow the race of a loyal servant who had saved him from assassination to be eradicated by anyone, not even someone as high up as Haman. Xerxes would soon see through Haman's plan.

• Perhaps more importantly, Zeresh was also reminded of Jewish history. The Jewish race had been in trouble time and time again and been threatened with annihilation, but God had saved them each time and was well-known as a protective, saving God, even among non-Jews. Everyone knew that the Jewish God was a force to be reckoned with. Why she only remembered this now and could not have warned Haman earlier, we don't know, but this incident seems to have jogged her memory and sent doom into the Haman household.

So we leave Haman being escorted to the next banquet with his wife's warning ringing in his ears. I am sure he was not looking forward to this banquet nearly as much the last one. What a difference a day makes!

Think tank

1. God works in mysterious ways. For Xerxes, he used insomnia.

Do you have nights when you just can't sleep? It may be that you are worrying about something, or just can't drift off. Spend that time with God either in prayer or in reading the Bible. It may be that God is trying to tell you something, even if it is just to spend more time with him.

2. Do you sometimes get frustrated with God when he does not sort out your problems the way you would like and when you would like?

Are you experiencing that feeling right now? Try to be patient, and trust him. Don't give up praying but remember that his timing is perfect.

3. Do you sometimes boast about things you have done or possessions you have? If so, you are not alone. We are all guilty of this at times. Don't get me wrong: there is nothing wrong with being excited about something like scoring a winning goal or coming first in a swimming race, but when you start thinking that you are the most important player in the team and that they would not have won without you, then you have a problem. Thank God for your ability or possessions, and try to remain humble. God can and may decide at any point to take this ability/possession away—these things are gifts and are not necessarily yours to keep. Who you are as a person, and what Jesus means to you, are far more important than what you can do or what you own.

' . . . Live as if Christ died for you today and will come for you tomorrow. '

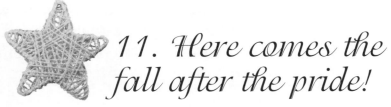

11. Here comes the fall after the pride!

Read Esther 7:1–10

Picture Haman, Esther and Xerxes sitting down to the second banquet. All three would have completely different hopes and fears for how the banquet would go.

Esther would have been very anxious about how her request would be taken and what the result would be. Remember, she was not just asking for a new dress. The lives of her people were on the line.

Haman would have been filled with nerves and dread. Although he still had no idea who Esther really was or what she wanted, I am sure he would have had his wife's words at the forefront of his mind!

Xerxes would have been very tired after his night of sleeplessness, but also intensely curious about what Esther's petition was all about. He was primed and ready, and Esther would have known that it was now or never. If she left it any longer, she would anger the king, and that was the last thing she wanted. God's timing was perfect.

Quite early on in the meal, I imagine, Xerxes again asked what Esther wanted and again offered her up to half his kingdom. This must have been quite reassuring to Esther, as her request was not that extreme.

I think that Esther would also have felt more confident about what she had to say next after Xerxes' offer.

Clever Esther (verses 1–4)

Again, we have to be impressed by how Esther phrased her request—or rather, impressed by how God guided her.

She starts straight away by being incredibly polite and humble in her speech and asking for her request to be granted only if it pleases the king.

She reminds the king of their close relationship by saying, 'If I have found favour with you'—in other words, if she has been a good and loyal queen.

She then asks for her life before the life of her people. This is not selfish of Esther at all, but very clever. She wants Xerxes to know that this order will affect his queen and will put her life in danger—not just the lives of some random people that he has had no direct contact with or affection for. His own wife is on death row. This order will have a direct, personal effect on the king himself.

She uses pretty much the same words—'destruction and slaughter and annihilation'—as were used in the order itself. Look back at Esther 3:13. She wants to make sure that there is no misunderstanding and that she cannot be accused of exaggerating her case.

She keeps the request humble and states that she would never bother the king if her people were simply being sold as slaves; obviously this is far worse.

She doesn't mention Haman as the author of this terrible order or put the blame on anyone. She waits for the king to ask, and it doesn't take long.

What a clever woman, but she was clearly guided by God in all she said and how she said it.

Message for today

Do you think God guides our speech today? I know that he does. Ask any preacher how he gives a sermon and one of the first things he will say is that he prays that God will give him the words to say. Yes, preachers do their study and preparation, but I have known preachers who, just before the sermon started, felt that God was guiding them to add to their sermon a subject that they had no previous intention of mentioning. Often there will have been someone in the congregation who needed to hear exactly that subject talked about. God definitely guides our speech if we ask him to. We just have to ask and to want to do his will, whatever that may entail … just like Esther.

Haman gets a shock *(verses 5–6)*

As soon as Esther used the specific words of his order,

Haman must have known the game was up, but what a shock to realize that the queen was a Jew! I don't think the king would have been particularly concerned as he had no idea which race was being slaughtered anyway. He would not have been appalled to realize that his wife was a Jew—but Haman now knew that he had picked the wrong race and the wrong God to war against. His ruin was coming far more quickly than he could have imagined.

Esther did not mince her words when Xerxes asked who had ordered the Jews' destruction. She called Haman the 'adversary and enemy', which he clearly was, but also described him as 'vile', which is an incredibly strong word to use. Again, it was true, but I think that, by using it, Esther was bringing home to Xerxes just how completely evil and untrustworthy Haman really was.

Remember, it would not have been just Haman who was shocked by this speech, but Xerxes too. Up until that moment, he was clueless about Haman and had thought Haman was completely trustworthy and noble. He had been blind to the real man, and it must have come as a terrible shock.

Haman makes his final mistake (verses 7–8)

When the pressure was on, Haman was not the brightest spark in the box!

The king was obviously furious for two reasons.

• His own queen's life had been threatened without his knowledge.

• His most trusted attendant, whom he had treated incredibly well, had not been honest with him. He thought he knew Haman, but now realized that he clearly did not know him at all.

I think the king also must have felt a bit stupid. He must have realized that he was partly to blame for not knowing which race his own wife belonged to, and for never having checked which race Haman wanted to annihilate before being so quick to grant his request.

I suspect that was why Xerxes needed to get some air (verse 7). He may have wanted to compose his thoughts and get a grip on himself before saying any more.

So, with the king out of the room, what does Haman do? OK, begging the queen for his life was not altogether a bad idea. It says in the passage that Haman knew that the king had decided 'his fate'—that he would put Haman to death. Haman clearly thought that his only chance was to try to get the queen to save him. I'm not sure that I wouldn't have made a run for it, although the chance of actually reaching the palace gates before the guards were alerted would have been very slim.

However, while begging, Haman seemed to think it was suddenly OK to invade the queen's personal space, and in his distress he then accidentally fell onto her couch. Not very clever at all. It was just not the done thing to get that close to the queen, not under any circumstance whatsoever, unless you were the king. Of course, it was at this exact moment that Xerxes returned, and he saw it all. (Coincidence or God's timing? You decide.)

I am sure that Haman never intended to get that close and personal to Esther, and I don't really think that Xerxes truly believed that Haman was trying to molest her, but he was in a rage and probably not thinking straight at that moment. But don't start feeling sorry for Haman. He brought all this on himself and was quite happy for thousands of men, women and children to be brutally murdered!

Haman's fate was sealed (verses 8–10)

In those days, when a person did wrong, if his or her face was covered it meant that the person had to die. Haman had lost big time.

Esther had clearly made an impression on a lot of people, including the eunuch, Harbona. He was a man who knew a lot about the goings on in the palace, as he knew about the gallows Haman had built and knew that he had intended to hang Mordecai on them. Harbona was also clearly a man you wanted on your side, and Esther had him on her side. As soon as Haman's face was covered, Harbona spoke up about the gallows. Harbona specifically mentioned that Mordecai was the one who had saved the king from the assassination plot. If the nails were not already in Haman's coffin, they surely were now, and were hammered in good and tight! The idea to hang Haman on his own gallows did not come from Esther at all.

Definition: *I would love to avoid this definition but we must be thorough. A* **eunuch** *was a man who had had his testicles forcibly removed. These men often worked in palaces, and I guess that they were treated in this way in order to prevent them from getting any ideas concerning the ladies in the palace, especially the queens they served regularly. Horrible, isn't it?*

So that's the story all wrapped up. The king had listened to Esther and believed her. The Jews' mortal enemy, Haman, was hanged. He could no longer cause any problems. So they all lived happily ever after.

NOT QUITE ...

We still have the tiny little problem of the order to annihilate the Jews. Just because the author of this order was now dead, it did not mean that the order no longer stood. Unfortunately, the order had been sealed by the king's ring and no one could revoke it ... not even the king himself. Was Haman still to have his way after all, even in death?

Message for today

It's amazing how things can radically change in the space of one day.

Dawn: Haman was one of the most envied men in the kingdom, being as close to the king as a man could possibly get.

Dusk: Haman was the most unenvied man in the kingdom, having been hanged on his own gallows at the king's order and now lying six feet under.

One day can make a huge difference, so let us make every day count. Your life can change radically in a moment, so be careful to do everything in a manner worthy of the gospel of Christ. One day, Jesus will come again. Let us be ready. Let us have no skeletons in our closets, as we can hide nothing from Jesus. Instead, try to live an honest life to please him in everything.

Here is a saying that my husband told me and which has really struck a chord with me:

Live as if Christ died for you today and will come for you tomorrow.

Think tank

1. Read Psalm 73:1–20. Do the words here remind you of anyone? It was written by a gentleman called

Asaph, but he clearly had people like Haman in his life too: people who seem to get away with murder, live a life of luxury and never seem to get what they deserve. There are evil people who never seem to have a worry in the world. In many countries there have been dictators who have tortured and killed many innocent people and who have died comfortably in their luxury bedrooms at a ripe old age. There are many thieves and murderers who never get caught.

For example: At the moment, I am living in South Africa, and while it is a beautiful country, it does have a problem with serious violent crime. The police have so much to try to deal with that many criminals simply get away with their crimes. It is very easy to get cynical.

Doesn't seem fair, does it? Why doesn't God judge them as he judged Haman? How is it that they get away with it?

HE WILL JUDGE THEM, AND THEY WILL NOT GET AWAY WITH IT.

It won't always happen in this life, but remember that this life is fleeting anyway. Believe me, these people will be judged in the next life. An eternity in hell is the worst punishment possible. And it will never end!

2. Remember that God is the one who judges, not us. Obviously, God has given those who run countries the right to judge people who break the law, but we do not have the right to judge others. We must concentrate on our own lives and try to please God in everything we do, which includes showing love to others. Leave the judging to him.

' . . . in the next world, in heaven, there will be no suffering, no poverty and no crying. '

12. Not over yet!

Read Esther 8:1–17

So the truth was finally out. Esther had revealed who she was and how she was related to Mordecai.

Haman would have been turning in his grave. Not only did Mordecai get presented with the king's signet ring that was Haman's until his downfall, but he was also put in charge of Haman's old estate.

Two of the most important things in Haman's life were now in the hands of a Jew, and not just any Jew, but Haman's mortal enemy.

Although we are near the end of the story, there is still one matter to attend to. Esther was not about to lie back, put her feet up and have a holiday. Her people were still in danger—which meant she was, too.

Esther's work was not yet done (verses 1–6)

Esther had successfully managed to get rid of Haman, which was a great triumph, but her job was not yet done. Nothing had really changed, and the order to annihilate the Jews still stood. So again she came into the presence of the king, but this time she did things slightly differently.

• Before she was even offered the sceptre, she pleaded with the king to save her people.

• There is no record of her waiting for the king to notice her and speak to her first.

• She fell at his feet weeping.

This was clearly against palace protocol, but Esther must have felt that the king would be understanding, and apparently he was, as he did offer the sceptre to her (verse 4).

I think this part of the story often takes a back seat. When people think of the story of Esther, they mostly think of Haman's downfall. I know I did before writing this book. That was the part I remembered more than anything else and, although that was the beginning of the end, it is this section here, not Haman's downfall, that is the real climax of the story. This is the scene that the whole story has been leading up to. This was the main issue that needed to be resolved from the start, and Esther's actions showed how important it was to her. She was desperate. Haman being out of the way was one thing, but her people's future was her primary concern.

Xerxes does not get involved (verses 7–8)

Esther asked for a further order to be written to overrule Haman's order of annihilation.

I still don't quite understand why Haman's first order could not simply be torn up. Surely the king was powerful enough to revoke any order.

I think he could have torn up the first order, but pride was getting in the way, as it had all along in the whole Persian Empire. To revoke an order would be to admit that the king had been wrong in the first place, and that would have shown weakness in the king—and weakness in a king could not be seen to exist. That is why this slightly odd rule, that no order sealed with the king's ring could be revoked, had come into being.

There had to be a way around it, and Xerxes knew that the only way to save face was for another decree to be written, this time on behalf of the Jews. By this point, I think that Xerxes was washing his hands of the whole affair. His speech in verses 7–8 almost suggests that he felt he had done enough by giving the estate to Esther and hanging Haman. Now it was up to Esther, and Mordecai who was with her, to come up with another decree. He would agree to have this decree signed with his ring too, so that it could not be revoked.

Message for today

Are we also guilty of not admitting when we are wrong, just like Xerxes and the whole of Persian royalty? Do we feel it is a sign of being weak?

For example: American President Clinton was quite a good example of this. During his presidency, a scandal broke out over the fact that he had been having an affair with one of the young girls in the White House. He denied the affair publicly for a long time, but eventually the evidence became too much and he did admit it on national TV and apologize. He was too proud to admit straight away that he had been wrong, and yet, if he had done so, I honestly don't think it would have developed into the public scandal that it became. Clinton was not a bad US president and he did a lot of good during his terms in office, but because of his denial of that event and then his eventual admission when he was caught out, people remember him more for this scandal than for any good he did.

Hopefully, the message is clear. If you have done wrong, admit it straight away. Don't be proud and hide from it, or pretend that it was nothing to do with you. It can make things ten times worse if you are too proud to admit it. Being able to apologize is a sign of strength, not weakness. If Xerxes had just decided to revoke the first law, a lot of bloodshed might have been avoided—but let's get back to the story.

Esther and Mordecai write the new order
(verses 9–12)

Remember, they could not revoke anything that was contained in the first order, so how were they going to sort this problem out?

Mordecai, in a wisdom that could only have come from God, wrote an order stating the following:

On the very day when the first order would be put into practice, the Jews were given the right

- to destroy, kill or annihilate any armed force of any nationality or province that might attack them
- to plunder the property of their enemies
- to assemble and protect themselves beforehand.

And this order was sealed with the king's ring so that it could not be revoked either.

This plan amazes me every time I read about it. I would never have thought of anything so clever. The Jews

115

were able to plan ahead and get ready for any attack. They were not given the right to initiate an attack, but were to defend themselves against anyone who attacked them. It would definitely make some people think twice about attacking the Jews now. They would be a force to be reckoned with. And, of course ... God would be with them all the way, just as he had been so far.

Let the celebrations begin! *(verses 13–16)*

Mordecai sent the order throughout the whole Persian Empire, to all 127 provinces and in every language used in the empire, so that no one would be in any doubt about what the order contained!

Clearly, it went down very well with the Jewish people. As it says in verse 16,

For the Jews it was a time of happiness and joy, gladness and honour.

They must have felt as if they had been rescued and given a lifeline from certain death. What an exciting day this must have been for them! They now had a chance.

Message for today

Do you see any parallels between the situation of the Jews then and that of all Christians today? Just like the Jews, all Christians were once facing certain death. There was no way we could save ourselves from our situation

and from hell. But Jesus provided a way and died for us so that we could be rescued and given the opportunity of life—an eternal life with him. Our death order has been lifted, thanks to Jesus.

I think back to the words I quoted from my husband in the last chapter:

Live as if Christ died for you today.

Too often, I think we lose track of what Jesus has done for us, and we get bogged down by the troubles of this world and the hassles of everyday life—and I fully include myself in this. If we really lived as if Jesus had died for us today, we would be excited about going to church and would sing hymns and songs meaning every word that we sing. He has rescued us from certain death—how amazing is that! Let us act as if we truly believe it, and be joyous in our praise of him and excited at what he has done for us—just as the Jews were in Esther's time.

What a witness! *(verse 17)*

Look at the last verse of chapter 8. Many people of other nationalities came to faith in the God of the Jews because of this event, because of fear.

I know some people would say that fear is not a good reason to convert. However, if you are a Christian, think about your conversion (if you have not yet made that step, think about the reason why you are looking into Christianity). If I am honest, I know that for me, fear was involved:

- fear of not going to heaven
- fear of going to an eternal hell
- fear of trying to get through life with no one to talk to who understands and can do something about the problems I face
- fear of not understanding why we are here and what the purpose of life is
- fear of not being able to deal with all the wrong things I do
- fear of rejecting an awesome and powerful God.

Fear was not the whole story, and it shouldn't be that in anyone's conversion. Love has the biggest part to play—it certainly did in my own conversion—but fear has its place and can definitely be the initial reason for people starting to take Christianity seriously. Remember, Christians follow a loving, gracious God, but he is also completely powerful and is to be taken extremely seriously.

We are now approaching D-Day, the thirteenth day of the twelfth month, which was called Adar. Would it all work out as Mordecai and the Jewish race were hoping and planning for? One thing was certain: it would be another day which would make a huge difference in their lives.

Think tank

1. Mordecai had stayed faithful to God and had been rewarded very nicely for his role in the Haman episode.

There is a movement called the 'prosperity gospel' which is followed by people who honestly believe that, if they do good in this world and are faithful Christians, they will get rewarded financially and with good health in this life. I am sure that they could use the book of Esther as an example, and it is true that there are also other people in the Bible who were rewarded materially by God. Abraham, Isaac and Job are three of these.

However, I do not believe that the Bible teaches the 'prosperity gospel' at all. Yes, Esther and Mordecai were rewarded financially, but you just have to look at the disciples and Paul in the New Testament and see that material blessing is not always the result of following God. Paul, Peter, Stephen and John the Baptist were all faithful Christian men, but they suffered greatly for the gospel and were all put to death for their faith.

My point is that godly men and women were never promised an easy time in this world. In fact, Jesus warned us that the opposite is more likely to happen. Yes, some faithful Christians are healthy and well-off, but it is not a certainty. What is certain is that in heaven, there will be no suffering or poverty. We will be with Jesus, and it will be one long, amazing celebration! That is what every Christian should be looking forward to—that is our promise for the future.

2. Look at your own attitude as you attend your church or youth group, or read the Bible or try to pray. Are you excited about what Jesus has done for you? Why not put the saying 'Live as if Christ died for you today and will come for you tomorrow' on your bedroom wall or mirror so that you will see it first thing in the morning and last thing at night. It will help to keep you focused on what is really important in this world.

' . . . God was on their side and working hard! Without him, it would have been a completely different and much more tragic story! '

13. Don't forget this!

Read Esther 9:1–10:3

So there was a huge battle, loads of people died, but the Jews won at the end of the day. End of story!

I am sure there are a lot of people who would sum up the last two chapters of Esther exactly like this, but I think it is important not to be too flippant about this thirteenth day of the twelfth month.

I think there are some very important things to note about this day, other than the fact that the Jews defeated their enemies.

No one could stand against them (9:1–17)

Although we are not told if there were any Jewish fatalities, the most important thing to learn from these two days is that clearly the Jews triumphed big time. In chapter 9 verse 2 we are told, 'No one could stand against them.'

So how did they win so convincingly?

God was on their side and working hard! Without him, it would have been a completely different and much more tragic story!

The killing was very selective (9:1–17)

It would have been an awful day for all concerned, including the Jews, and if you read chapter 9 quickly and see the numbers of those killed, you might think that the Jews had gone on a rampage, but the writer of the book is very careful to point out that it was only the people who came to attack the Jews who were killed.

READ VERSE 1: '... the Jews got the upper hand over those who hated them ...'

READ VERSE 2: 'The Jews assembled ... to attack those seeking their destruction.'

The only people killed were those who attacked the Jews first. It was all in self-defence. There is no mention of women and children being put to death. Remember, Haman's original order did allow the killing of women and children, but the Jews appear to have had compassion and only killed the men who were actually attacking them.

No plunder taken (9:1–17)

'Plunder' refers to possessions or goods taken by force in a battle. This was also allowed in the order sent by Mordecai, but in verses 10 and 15 it is clearly stated that 'they did not lay their hands on the plunder'. This emphasizes again that the killing was purely in self-defence. There was no ulterior motive and get-rich-quick scheme.

The number of casualties was actually quite small (9:1–17)

If you add up the numbers given, 75,810 men were killed during the two days of fighting. It sounds a lot—and it was a lot—but remember, this was the number throughout the 127 provinces. Look back to Chapter 1 to remind yourself of how big this land was. That number of casualties was actually relatively small, probably because the nobles and governors of the provinces helped the Jews, as they were scared of Mordecai (see 9:3; translated literally, it means that they were scared of Mordecai's powerful God!).

It could have been a lot worse if:

• the Jews had not been allowed to defend themselves in the first place

• or if the Jews had gone ahead and killed anyone they pleased, including the women and children.

War is horrible, no matter the rights or wrongs of any side, but this really was the only outcome that could have caused as little suffering as possible.

Why the extra day of killing in the citadel of Susa?

As you would have noted in verse 13, Esther asked the king for the Jews in Susa to be given an extra day to kill those who came to attack them.

It seems, on the surface, that this extra day was completely unnecessary, and that Esther was being quite vindictive in asking Xerxes for this extra day for the Jews in the capital to 'defend' themselves. It also seems quite a gory thing for Esther to ask for the already dead ten sons of Haman to then be hanged in public—but there was a reason behind both requests.

THE EXTRA DAY. Esther's concern, I imagine, was that Haman would have had allies in the city who would have wanted to seek revenge, especially after Haman's ten sons had also been killed. And she was right. If this had not been the case, the Jews would not have had to kill anyone that day.

THE PUBLIC HANGING. This would have made a horrible sight, but it would have been an unforgettable warning to anyone having further thoughts about attacking the Jews. It was a message to say, 'This could be you!'

A celebration—Lest we forget! (9:18–10:3)

Mordecai became a very important man, and as we read in Esther chapter 10, he was soon promoted to second in rank to Xerxes. After the bloodshed was over and the Jews had survived, he wrote letters to all the Jews throughout the provinces to recommend that the fourteenth and fifteenth days of the month of Adar be celebrated every year and be added to the current Jewish festivals. It was to be called **'The feast of Purim'**.

'Pur' is the Hebrew word for 'lot'. Remember, Haman cast a lot ('pur') to see which day was going to be the day for the annihilation of the Jews.

It is awful to think of people celebrating after so much bloodshed, but they were not celebrating the deaths but their own rescue from certain death … there is a difference!

For example: Think back to what you have learnt about the two world wars, especially the Second World War. If you have seen any news clips about the day the war was declared to be over, you will remember seeing people celebrating in the streets. They were not celebrating the number of lives lost on the side of their enemies, but the fact that there would be no more killing on their side and that their men would be coming home.

This feast of Purim is still celebrated among Jews today and is a very happy time, when Jews exchange presents, give to the poor and remember how God delivered them from the hands of Haman through Esther and Mordecai.

Message for today

How often do you ask God for help in some area or to intervene in some way, and he does—but you then forget to thank him? More than that, you forget that he even helped you in the first place, but carry on regardless. I know that I am guilty of this more often than I care to admit. God does so much for us, in small ways as well as big. Let us take a leaf out of Mordecai's book and make a concerted effort to remember and be very grateful!

So we leave Esther and Mordecai in a good place. God's will was done, and the Jewish people were rescued.

Note: It would seem that Xerxes got away with the whole episode even though he clearly made

some serious mistakes. However, we do know that his downfall came later, when he was murdered and his throne taken over. We don't know what happened to Esther or Mordecai, but if we are Christians, one day we will find out. Personally, I can't wait to ask Esther in heaven!

Think tank

1. If you have a Jewish friend, ask him or her how Jews celebrate Purim today.

2. Can you think of days in the year when Christians celebrate special events? Write them down, and write down the reason for celebration or remembrance.

3. It is all too easy to forget all that God does for us personally. Try writing a diary of all the things you have asked God for, and then each week look back to see how he answered your prayers. This helps you to remember how much he has answered your prayers (even if not in the way you hoped) and reminds you to thank him for it.

Titles in this series

Ruth   128 pages
More than a love story
Clark, Helen
978-1-84625-078-1
The story of the God who loved Ruth and
had a plan for her life, applying principles to
younger readers today.

Simon Peter   112 pages
The training years
Clark, Helen
978-1-84625-157-3
The story of Peter as disciple and how God
had a plan for his life, applying principles to
younger readers today.

Simon Peter   112 pages
Challenging times
Clark, Helen
978-1-84625-158-0
The story of Peter the apostle and how God
had a plan for his life, applying principles to
younger readers today.

Esther   128 pages
God's invisible hand
Clark, Helen
978-1-84625-204-4
The story of Queen Esther and how God had a
plan for her life, applying principles to younger
readers today.